The 5 W's of Wealth Creation

Keys to lasting wealth

Elizabeth Benjamin

Copyright © 2015 Elizabeth Benjamin

The right of Elizabeth Benjamin to be identified as the Author of the work has been asserted by him in accordance with the Copyright, Designs and Patent Act 1988.

All rights reserved. No part of this publication may be reproduced, stored in a retrieval system or transmitted, in any form or by any means, without the prior written permission of the author, be otherwise circulated in any form of binding or cover, other than that in which it is published. A CIP catalogue record for this title is available from the British Library.

ISBN: 978-1-910090-41-1

Book cover design and layout by: www.madeforministry.co.uk

Printed by: www.madeforministry.co.uk

CONTENTS

Dedication	4
Foreword	5
Chapter One - Wealth Creation	9
Chapter Two - Financial Wealth	15
Chapter Three - Why?	19
Chapter Four - Who?	33
Chapter Five - What?	37
Chapter Six - Financial Habits and Housekeeping	45
Chapter Seven - How do I get there?	53
Chapter Eight - Nuggets of Wealth Creation	65
Chapter Nine - Actions for Lasting Wealth	85
Chapter Ten - Workbook	89

Dedication

I dedicate this book to my dearest mother who has been, and continues to be, a rock on which I can depend. It is because of her love and patience that I have been able to become the person that I am.

Mother, you are an inspiration to me and I am thankful for all of the sacrifices you have made. It is through your love and investment in my wellbeing that I can stand where I stand today.

It always goes without saying – but I would like to acknowledge my husband, children and family. Your strength and help has contributed to my development and the success of every project I take on.

Finally, I would also like to dedicate this book to Theresa, my best friend, who has remained loyal and supportive throughout the years. This book would not have been possible without you.

Foreword

I am an ordinary individual from a modest, working class background. Over the years, as a working mother of four, I have juggled a variety of jobs along with my family commitments. Although I settled into a steady career, I believed there was more to my existence than just being financially 'comfortable'. I desired security and decided to take action by creating the kind of wealth that would not only meet my needs, but also make an impact in the lives of other people and create a legacy. This decision prompted me to ask myself some uncomfortable but honest questions about why I had such a strong desire for financial success. Was it greed? Was I trying to cover an underlying fear or did I truly desire to help others as well as myself?

I began by making some fundamental changes. The questions that I asked myself and the answers I discovered eventually led me to write this book about my journey to financial freedom and what I now term as a recipe for wealth creation.

Whilst our wants may come packaged in different shapes and sizes, financial freedom is something we all desire. Wealth is about so much more than just money. I define wealth as a plentiful supply of a good thing. This means wealth can be widened to encompass financial, physical, social, emotional and spiritual abundance. A person that is truly wealthy will experience increase and growth in all five realms.

Financial freedom may look different for each individual but ultimately it is a tool that ensures us more 'free' time and plentiful choice. For most, the desire is nothing but a daydream that will never come to fruition. The hope for abundant wealth goes hand-in-hand with the "I wish…" and "If only…" clichés of life.

What if I told you that your desire for financial freedom need not be a wish? What if I said that financial freedom is a realistic and achievable goal you can attain? Whilst it may sound too good to be true, financial freedom can be realised. This is not a get-rich-quick scheme or super-fast money making gimmick, nor is it a motivational pep talk. By simply establishing some fundamental truths, you can find your way to financial freedom.

Did you know that the Bible mentions money more than any other single topic? Our attitude towards money determines whether wealth is a blessing or a curse. The truths taken from the Bible and noted in this book are exactly that – truths. They can be beneficial to all. I have referred to the Bible at various points and in specific chapters. As a Christian, I cannot separate my achievements from my faith as they go hand in hand.

In this book, I share the five W's of wealth creation; five essential questions that must be asked, answered and settled by anyone who wants to create lasting wealth. I'm sure you will find it interesting that your journey to financial freedom starts with these simple, yet essential, questions:

Why?
What?
Who?
When?
Where?

Every budding inventor asks why, what, who, when and where - because in order to find the correct remedy we must first ask the right questions. The 'why' is usually the ultimate motivator that propels the inventor to create. Behind every successful invention, creation, system, service or lifestyle – there is always a 'why' question. The answer may not be immediately obvious, but once found, results follow. The recipe for creating lasting wealth is embedded in accurate questioning, finding the right solutions and then applying them because good solutions to quality questions will ensure longevity.

The principles I share in this book have helped me build a successful multimillion-pound real estate portfolio using a £5,000 bank loan to build a £15 million asset portfolio. I was able to retire early from a 9-5 job role, spend more quality time with my family and finally pursue things that were close to my heart. I now offer much sought after advice, assistance and mentoring to likeminded individuals who aspire to achieve financial freedom. If I can do it, so can anyone.

Knowledge without understanding and application simply becomes useless information. The key is in the knowing but the doing is what puts the key to use and unlocks the door. The lessons in this book must be put into operation. You must ask, plan, prepare and act (APPA). I truly believe what separates those who create lasting wealth from those who don't, lies in the questions they ask and their approach to finding the right answers then acting on them.

The 5 W's of Wealth Creation is a practical workbook and must be used as such in order to fully reap the benefits. It is important that you do not simply treat it as a book. Instead, view it as a manual or study guide that has been designed to accompany you on your wealth creation journey. At the end of every chapter take time to pause and endeavour to answer the questions. Don't just go through the motions – use the questions to draw up a plan of action and then begin to walk the plan out step by step.

With wealth comes responsibility. By challenging belief systems, changing preconceptions and applying identified principles both wealth and financial freedom can be attained. However, anyone aspiring to create lasting, stable and sustainable wealth in any area of their life must understand that with each degree of wealth comes a greater degree of duty, influence and responsibility; money is only as functional or serviceable as the person that controls it.

I hope *The 5 W's of Wealth Creation* will encourage anyone who works hard, yet hasn't been able to create the wealth they dream of. If, like me, you have asked yourself; "Why do I always have more month than money?" - "Why does it always feel as though I'm playing catch-up where my finances are concerned?" - "Why can't I spend my time doing the things that really matter?" then this book is for you. Financial freedom is possible. I have no doubt that as you read on, the words in this book will lead you to your road of wealth creation.

Chapter One
Wealth Creation

Wealth Creation

Wealth is a choice. Everyone on the planet has the potential to obtain wealth and have an abundance to cater for their needs as well as help meet the needs of others.

There are two key components required when creating wealth:

1) *Asking quality questions:*

The right questions will elicit the right information.

2) *Sowing and reaping:*

Everything that happens in terms of your wealth creation success will be determined by your actions - you get what you put in.

Wealth creation can be likened to each of the three scenarios below:

Scenario One – The Farmer: In its most basic form, wealth creation is very similar to the process of farming. When a farmer sows seeds, he expects a bountiful harvest (provided he has tended to and maintained the seeds as they grow). The farmer plans, prepares, manages and monitors his investment to produce a bountiful harvest. The process that the farmer undertakes can be likened to wealth creation because seeds are the opportunities that are available to us all. The harvest is the income expected after the work is complete and an investment of time has been sown 'nurturing' the product to ensure a return.

Scenario Two – The Athlete: If an athlete desires to achieve success then discipline is essential. Like athletes, wealth creators are running a race to obtain a prize or reward. Mastering wealth creation requires a focus of mind, determination and good planning. It is not a sprint; it is a marathon and preparation is key.

Scenario Three – The Traveler: Whenever you go on a journey, the items you take are determined by where you go and what you plan on doing whilst there. For the traveler, a destination is determined and then appropriate planning and preparation, relating to the chosen destination, begins. Choice of clothes, relevant paperwork, mode of transport and available resources are all essential elements required to reach the chosen destination and ensure that the experience is joyous and profitable. Wealth creation is your chosen destination and the choices you make will determine the success of your journey and how quickly you arrive.

What thoughts do the above scenarios invoke?

_____
_____
_____
_____
_____
_____

Hopefully the listed scenarios will have helped you begin thinking about some key questions:

- Why do farmers sow large quantities of seed rather than just enough to feed their family?

- Why does an athlete compete for a reward?

- Why do you desire to be financially free?

- Why are you thinking about wealth creation?

The commonality within each scenario is passion. The farmer, the athlete and the traveler all have a sense of passion for their tasks which supports their desire to achieve. Each individual must have a desire to succeed and accomplish whatever they set out to do. You must approach your goals with avidity and pursue each one with dogged tenacity. Your desire must go beyond meeting your own needs. The biggest and most successful dreamers are those who pursue things that will ultimately better or help others. The more people you are able to impact, the stronger the legacy you will leave behind. Wealth creators do not simply think about themselves and their retirement – they are able to envisage the generations that will follow after them. When approached from this perspective, creating wealth becomes much more than a hobby, game or desire. It evolves into a person's aim to make a stamp on the world.

Motivation must be established and understood because it is what will drive you. Coupled with passion, it will ensure that you go all the way - even when you face obstacles. With the right motivation you will have the ability to break through barriers.

A significant number of successful athletes go through periods of injury. A farmer's crops may be adversely impacted by bad weather or other external conditions and a traveler can often face delays in reaching their desired location. Most of today's successful entrepreneurs have faced a variety of hurdles in their quest for success. The difference is, they considered the obstacles as setbacks and not immovable roadblocks that could not be overcome. That's what made them successful. They pressed on, endured the pain and focused on the joy of reaching their destination.

You are only able to focus on the end goal if you have a clear vision. Along with identifying your passion and motives, you must have a clear picture of your end goal.

How do you start?

Creation requires a hypothetical seed to be sown by its creator. Your seeds may come in the form of ideas, concepts, information, finances or education; this is not an exhaustive list. The important point is that the concept of 'sowing seed' to create is understood.

WEALTH CREATION
Chapter One

Wealth cannot be created without action. In order to sow your seed you must take action and *do* something. Seed sowing will require work, effort and exertion on your part. You must begin to sow your seeds no matter how small or insignificant they may seem.

The next step is acknowledging that sacrifices must be made on your journey to creating wealth. The single mindedness, the determination, the self-discipline and the denial of some temporary rewards must all take center stage to ensure you arrive at your planned destination.

It's okay to think big, but start small - you will grow from there. Start with the resources that you are able to spare no matter how meager they seem. What do you have at your disposal right now? You may say nothing, but there is always something; remember *you* are your greatest asset. Utilise opportunities, networks and relationships that may prove beneficial to your cause.

Ask yourself the following questions:

- What seeds have I sown towards my wealth creation?

_____

_____

_____

- What disciplines can I introduce to ensure that my seeds grow and flourish?

_____

_____

_____

- What tools / resources do I need and what do I currently have available or accessible?

  _____
  _____
  _____

- Have I challenged myself to address possible difficulties I may encounter?

  _____
  _____
  _____

If wealth is not a science but an art, it should follow that everyone on earth can create the wealth of their dreams. Why then does it seem that so many who desire to create wealth are unable to do so? Read on and discover the answer.

Chapter Two

Financial Wealth

People are unable to create wealth because they do not understand it and as a result they misuse it. Before you can attain lasting wealth it is important to understand what true wealth really is. If you fail to understand its definition then you will fail to understand its purpose and abuse will be inevitable.

Most people define financial wealth as having lots of money, resources or assets. They associate wealth with being well to do, prosperous and comfortable. Wealthy people own their own home, or homes, outright. They have several cars and can take holidays to tropical and exotic locations frequently or at a moment's notice.

There are those that define wealth as having more money than you 'need'. This definition can be hard to grasp because the concept of 'need' varies drastically from person to person. To some wealth equates to people not having to work or those that are grouped in the top tax rates, which kicks in at £150,000 a year in the UK and $379,151 in the US.[1]

A recent survey by UBS (Union Bank of Switzerland), in 2013, stated that most investors defined being 'wealthy' as having a minimum of $5 million—with at least $1 million of that in cash. [2]

The UBS *Investor Watch* asked 4,450 investors, worth $5 million or more, whether they considered themselves wealthy. A full 60% of those surveyed said yes, while 28% said they did not consider themselves wealthy. [3]

Half of the respondents said being wealthy means having "no financial constraints on activities." 10% defined wealth as "not having to work again." The majority of those surveyed believed that being wealthy does not just mean having millions in investments or assets, but it also means having plenty of cash on hand to handle any expense or emergency. [4]

A significant number of people consider themselves to be 'rich' because they live in a detached house, they reside in a nice affluent neighbourhood, have a couple of cars on the forecourt and perhaps own a boat or can afford to hire a yacht for family holidays. As glamorous and impressive as this may seem, the picture becomes less desirable when you realise that they also have several credit cards and are on their second or third mortgage in addition to the re-mortgage of their main home. As they are able to make monthly repayments on their mortgages, credit cards and loans and still have some money left over to live on, they think they are well off or even comfortably rich.

I have a totally different opinion on this; **you simply cannot claim to have real financial wealth if you are in debt.**

My definition of financial wealth mirrors a reply to some research conducted by Forbes on the 400 wealthiest people in 2013. When each was asked the question: **"What is the single most important key to building wealth?"** 75% of them answered: **"Live debt free".** [5]

This answer sums up the definition of wealth. That is a hard pill to swallow for many, especially in this buy now - pay later culture that has become the norm for the majority of society. A person that is debt free and owes nothing can truly live in a state of abundance. When you no longer have a mortgage on your home; are able to pay cash for your cars, children's school fees and house hold bills; give generously and still have savings, cash in reserve for emergencies, cater for your retirement and leave a handsome inheritance for your loved ones – you are financially wealthy.

Financial wealth means you are able to meet your day-to-day needs without the accumulation of debt. It is not just about being comfortable, financial wealth is an overflowing state where your surplus can make a significant difference in the lives of others. True financial wealth means you do not panic if interest rates rise or if you lose your job because your income is not determined by a pay slip or the state of the economy. Are you beginning to get the picture?

What does living debt free look like for you?

_____
_____
_____
_____

It does not matter how much you earn or how much money is coming in if you keep asking the question 'what if...' "What if I lose my job?" - "What if interest rates rise?" - "What if my loan agreements change?"

Answer the following questions to assess your level of financial wealth:

1. Are you wealthy by the definition described above?

2. If you lost your job today, could you meet all your financial obligations for the next 3 – 6 months?

3. If you are a buy-to-let landlord with a second or third mortgage and your property becomes vacant for 3 months would you be able to meet all related financial obligations?

4. Do you want to live in a state of abundance?

If the answer to the last question is 'yes' then there are more questions you must ask and more solutions you must find before you can begin to build sustainable wealth.

Chapter Three
Why?

So you want to be wealthy? Then the first question you must ask yourself is 'why?' In essence, it is this one question that will lead to many answers.

Answer the three 'why' questions below and implement them into your plans for success.

The mindset that you are in when you answer the 'why' questions will determine your approach and the quality of your answers. Do not look at your future based on today. The needs and desires you have now, will not be the same in ten years. With that said, think with the future at the forefront of your mind; have a perspective that looks at things in light of long term results.

It is important that you take the time to really think about your answers. Be honest with yourself, do not just write down something because it seems like a good answer or sounds charitable.

Honest answers will ensure that any underlying concerns or possible challenges are brought to the surface.

1. Why do you desire to create more wealth?

_____
_____
_____
_____

2. Why do you want to become financially independent?

_____
_____
_____
_____

3. Why now?

_____
_____
_____
_____

A significant number of people never succeed in creating anything because their 'why' is not strong enough to push through all the obstacles. As a result, they doubt themselves, give up and fail.

The answer to your 'why' is a personal thing. It can only be answered by understanding who you really are, knowing what you value, realising your worth and acknowledging your belief system. This may sound simple, but it is the simplicity that makes it work. Within you is the fuel that can feed your motivations and ensure you go all the way to achieve your dreams.

Once you have answered 'why' you can begin a course of action. You will know where to start and have a clearer idea of who to approach for assistance, what actions to take and when etc.

It will be difficult to harness lasting wealth unless you answer the 'why' question at the onset of your journey. If answered correctly, your answer to the question should lead you to discover your destination. This will become your fuel, your motivator and your cause. It will give you a focal point – something to hold, even if things go wrong, because you have a target. Your answer to the 'why' question will get you through the journey to creating your wealth or any other goal you are striving to reach.

Go back and take a look at your answers. Are they so strong that you are willing to keep digging the well until you find water? Does your reason for financial freedom outweigh your immediate needs and aim to help others? Is your determination strong enough for you to deny yourself temporary enjoyment?

I believe that everything and everyone has a purpose – there is a reason for the creation or existence of each and every single thing on the face of the earth. Cars were created to be driven and pens were invented to be written with. God created the world and sacrificed His Son on the cross because of His love for mankind. Nothing that is worth anything is ever without purpose. Your purpose in life is something you must find, follow and fulfill in order to become a wealth creator.

Similarly, for you to create lasting wealth you must have the frame of mind that literally screams: "I must do this because…" "I cannot go on like this because…", "I have to be healthy because…", "I must improve my relationships because…" "I must have a successful career because…" Many of us have heard the saying "average is the enemy of excellence". You must set your mind to have a burning desire to create wealth. Mediocre or average attitudes simply will not do. You must never become complacent or comfortable with your current state. Always strive to become more because then you can do more, have more and achieve more.

Within the mind of every human, God has hidden the wealth of the world. Ultimately, the earth is the Lords but He has given the world to His children. [6] Nothing happens without the permission of the mind. Our minds are powerful. We should ensure that we exercise our minds more than our muscles because whatever is thinkable is achievable. A poor mind cannot create an abundance of wealth. Poor mindsets equal empty pockets!

The parable of the prodigal son [7] tells the story of a young man who prematurely requests his share of the family estate then squanders his inheritance on reckless living. When famine arose, he had nothing left and was so hungry he was willing to eat the food that was fed to the pigs. That was his 'why' moment. He had sunk so low that he considered eating with pigs. He asked himself the question and it was only when he answered it that he realised he had to change. He could not continue to live the way he was, knowing he was worth much more. He knew his father loved him, he realised his mistake and knew he had to change. The prodigal son realised that even the servants in his father's house lived in a better state. Answering 'why' led him to action – which led to the questions of 'what' he needed to do, 'who' was available to help him, 'where' things would take place and 'when' it would all happen. The prodigal son went through the following process as he asked himself the foundational questions:

Why – Why am I here? (Even the servants at my father's house are treated better)

What – What can I do? (I desire change)

Who – Who can I go to? (My father can help)

When – When can the change I desire take place? (Now)

Where – Where must I go? (To my father)

Whilst this is a highly simplified outline of the questioning process, it does provide a summarised example about the five W's of wealth creation. Until you can ask yourself why you want what you want, you will not be able to create lasting wealth; be it financial, physical, social or otherwise. Although there will be some universal questions, the majority will be specific to you and they must be answered with a deep sense of conviction to achieve the legacy that you so desperately want. The truth can be hard to face sometimes, but it must be a sincere evaluation – so be honest!

In my experience as a financial adviser and debt counselor, most people know what they want. It often ranges from things like financial freedom, to losing or gaining weight, to getting married and having children. However, the 'why' is usually assumed. People rarely ask themselves why they want what they want. Instead, they rush off to find solutions without building the conviction needed to achieve and sustain their desires. As a result, their journeys are usually short lived.

Weight loss is an excellent example. Have you ever noticed that the people who successfully lose weight and keep it off are the ones who have very strong reasons for doing it in the first place? Their reasons far outweigh any problems, challenges or temptations they may face. Several years ago, a colleague of mine lost 10st through diet and exercise in a desperate bid to save her life, as doctors had given her just months to live. She was in a desperate state and there were only two options presented to her; life or death. She chose to live. Her reason 'why' went beyond her 'here and now'. She wanted to live because she desired to see her children have children. If that 'why' was to become a reality then she would need to:

Change her diet: that was her 'What'

Get understanding by obtaining information from dieticians, doctors and other sources: that was her 'Who'

Make changes immediately: that was her 'When'

Now, you may say that wealth creation and financial freedom are not that serious. It is true that people who fail to achieve financial freedom do not die, but the journey must be approached with a similar mentality if you are to ever achieve your goal. Complacency must become your enemy; you must refuse to settle for average.

Your 'why' must transcend your hear and now. It must go beyond the present and have an eternal quality to it. What I mean by this is that things that are usually of any real value or significance have a sense of longevity to them. They are not short-lived. I am not talking merely about time but rather about concept, perception and value.

Is your 'why' strong enough? Has your 'why' come as a result of the pain of having to work for an organisation where you are unappreciated, overworked and underpaid? Are you working long hours and still not able to afford holidays or spend quality time with your family? Do you desire to wipe away the shame of your past? Do you want to break the poverty chain that existed throughout your childhood? Do you fear the pain of pigsty living like the prodigal son? Has living on the top floor of a council flat in a rundown neighbourhood spurred you on?

You may or may not resonate with some of the possible 'whys' above, as your questions will always be influenced by your life experiences. Whatever the reason; it has to be real to you and it has to be meaningful to you personally.

The reasons I described were real life situations of several people who have been able to break the chain of poverty and create lasting wealth. These people have gone on to empower and influence their generation through innovation and finance. They have surpassed the level of meeting only their needs and achieved things that outweigh material wealth by giving back charitably and making a positive impact to the world around them.

Wealth does not have to divide. When used correctly and responsibly money can be one of the greatest tools. It aids in providing the solution to many things on this earth. How you view money is a very important part to your wealth creation journey. The money must not be your focal point. That may sound ironic, as we are talking about financial freedom, but bear with me. The operative word in financial freedom is 'freedom'. When you have enough money, you no longer have to worry about bills or debt and have enough surplus to help others - it liberates you in other areas. It must never just be about the money. It must always be about what you can do with the money. Your focus must be on what opportunities are available and how you can utilise finances to maximise the possibilities presented to you.

Although I grew up in a loving and stable environment, my parents were like most average parents in our community-oriented culture. They were not just responsible for looking after their own children; they were also responsible for the wellbeing of extended family members. This meant we lived in a very crowded house. I grew accustomed to landlords who looked down on my parents if the rent was late. Despite working hard, they sometimes struggled to pay our school fees and had to borrow money from friends.

It fascinates me that as human beings we are wired to like nice things. No one has to be taught to enjoy comfortable surroundings, warm clothing or good food. The ability to acknowledge beautiful and pleasant things comes naturally to us. As a family, we ate cheap food because it was what we could afford and although I was happy, I hated the situation. I grew up with a strong determination within me to break the poverty chain I had experienced. Living from hand to mouth characterised my childhood and I did not want it to continue in my adult life. My desire to break free and create my own wealth was all consuming for me. Seeing my parents struggling to go to work, even through ill health was especially hard. I wanted to be wealthy enough to build them a house and ensure that they no longer had to struggle.

When I turned 19, I was given the opportunity, through a government award, to study in the United Kingdom. I arrived in England with just a suitcase to my name and had no other support. I took on several low paid part time jobs to support myself through my studies. It was a very stretching time, and it was at this point that my reason 'why' began to evolve.

I was living in a council flat on the second floor and one day, I went to pick up my nine year old daughter from school but she was not there. My husband was away working abroad. I looked everywhere for her and asked teachers and other parents in the school if they had seen her but no one could help me. Four hours had passed. By this point I was in total panic and contacted the police. Their response was to tell me to wait a further 6 hours before reporting her missing. I was distraught; I went back home and prayed to God, asking Him to help me find her. Just before the 6 hours was up, I went out again looking for my daughter and a lady, seeing my distress, asked me what the matter was. I explained that my daughter was missing. She asked for her description and when I told her, said she had seen her with a woman and another child. She could not tell me precisely where the woman lived but said it might be three or four streets away – pointing in a particular direction. Although her directions were vague and hazy, to say the least, they were all I had. The hours that had gone by, felt like months. I was desperate to find my daughter and willing to act on any information.

I went to the fourth street from mine and started knocking on the doors of people's homes. As I continued down the street, I heard faint sounds of children playing in the back garden of a specific house. I knocked on the door and was casually greeted by a woman asking if I had come to collect my daughter. I vaguely recognised the woman and realised I had seen her on several occasions at the school gates waiting to collect her children. I did not know that our children were friends until that day. I was both relieved and angry. I told her that I had been looking for my daughter for hours and had not given her permission to go to her friend's house.

On the way home, I chastised my daughter and asked why she left the school grounds without telling me. She replied that she wanted to play in a garden and her friend said she could come and play in hers. Her friend's mother had tried to call me but there was no answer, I later found out that she had an incorrect number for me.

That night was my 'prodigal son' moment. I told myself that I had to get out of living in a council high rise. I remembered the look on my mother's face whenever she was unwell but still had to go to work. It stirred the same emotions as the image of my daughter's face, streaming with tears, crying for a garden to play in. Like all parents I want the best for my children, I began to think about their future and the memories I wanted to leave them with. I did not want them to experience the same things I had as a child. Enough was enough. My reasons 'why' were so strong that I pushed myself to initiate a plan for my journey to create wealth. For me it was about so much more than having a garden to play in. That garden represented opportunity, it represented choice and it made me realise that I wanted to provide my children with both.

I started to think about my 'what' questions, which naturally led me to my 'who', 'where' and 'when' questions.

I knew I wanted to buy my own home with a garden that my family could enjoy. I also knew that in order to do that, I had to have assets – investments which would give me a passive income that wouldn't require me to work three jobs just to make ends meet or jeopardise quality time with my family. I also wanted to have a surplus for other endeavours too.

Even when things were tough, I stood my ground and endured it because my 'why' was strong enough. I was willing to keep digging my well until I created my wealth.

You do not want your decision for change to be an emotional one. Our emotions change continuously and are not usually the best thing to propel a person into action because eventually emotions change and momentum is lost. The incident with my daughter added to my 'why'. Whilst it was not the pivotal factor, it did propel me into action. Sometimes that is what it takes for us to act; something has to happen. Now, there is nothing wrong with an experience, situation or circumstance that encourages a person to act but the wisest thing to do is act not based on your circumstances but based on what you know. Circumstances change but the knowledge you acquire, if done correctly, will only grow and expand – it will evolve.

The next thing I did was look for the right person that could help me. I was able to enquire of a friend how he went about owning his home. I also spoke to the council about the process of buying an ex-council property. I registered with various agents in the area and received frequent property updates. I started a one year saving plan and any excess money (which basically meant every penny that did not go to food, bills or rent) went into a savings account. Within two years I was able to put down the deposit for my first home. The council told me that I could be offered a 60% discount of the flat I lived in or receive an incentive to relocate. I decided to take the incentive simply because it provided the opportunity to move to a more affluent area where property values were on the rise. It was a fresh start.

Although I was grateful for the opportunity of stepping onto the ladder of home ownership by getting a mortgage, I soon realised that I was at the bottom of the ownership ladder whilst banks and mortgage lenders were at the top. There is difference between possession and ownership; a mortgage did not give me full ownership as the bank had overall control and so I remained a servant to the lender – so to speak. I felt as though getting a mortgage to buy a home would be the same as exchanging one landlord for another. I desired to own a home outright. I did not want to owe a bank or anyone else for that matter, so I continued to dig.

It was partly my own state of desperation that led me to ask the 'why' question. With a mortgage, even when interest rates would rise, I had to get a second job to meet the increased repayments. I felt as though I was just barely hanging on - until the storm passed.

At the time of making the decision to become a wealth creator I was driving a run down Micra car and there was pressure from friends to change it and buy something newer and trendier. There were comments, albeit made in jest, asking when I was going to change my car to match my 'status'. Some were astounded that I had not yet taken my

WHY?
Chapter Three

children to Disneyland Florida, as it was a popular holiday destination at the time. You see, my 'why' meant I had to prioritise. I knew I had to sacrifice temporary enjoyment for lasting wealth. I knew that buying an expensive car at the time would mean I had to continue to serve the mortgage lender for a longer period. It would mean I'd probably have to buy a new car mostly on credit or hire purchase. A car, in itself, would have been a depreciating asset and would not have taken me to my wealth creation destination. I knew that the 'vehicle' I needed to possess was an appreciating asset.

Questions for reflection

Complete the following questions and then review and reflect on your answers.

- Is your 'why' strong enough to outlast your immediate circumstances or needs?

_____
_____
_____
_____

- Are you in the right mind frame for wealth creation?

_____
_____
_____
_____

- Are you willing to temporarily deny yourself of things that are not necessary or essential?

  _____
  _____
  _____
  _____

- How do you plan to use financial wealth to help others?

  _____
  _____
  _____
  _____

- Has your 'why' for wealth creation failed you in the past? If so, you may want to think about what is different this time and identify a 'why' that is long lasting as well as genuine.

  _____
  _____
  _____
  _____

Remember, we all have power to create wealth. What will separate you from others is understanding that your desire for wealth creation must be stronger than a simple wish or want. It must be purposeful!

Chapter Four
Who?

Have you heard the saying: "Your network will determine your net worth" and vice versa? Well, it is a true statement.

"If you don't know what to do you should know who does." This means if you know _why_ you want to create wealth and you are passionate and in the right frame of mind, it should naturally progress you to _who_ is best to help and guide you. This will be followed by or coupled with _what_ to do, how to do it and _where_ and _when_ to do it. Whilst the order of questions are not mutually exclusive, they must all be answered to ensure that you are not wasting resources, time and energy on various schemes that will not work or do not last and fail to take you to your destination.

Financial wealth is not acquired through pyramid schemes that are short lived and costly in the long run. If you decide to create lasting wealth, then you must be able to turn to someone who has already travelled that road and who is where you aspire to be.

Mentorship is helpful. You are able to avoid many pitfalls because those that have gone before you have tried, tested and proven methods that work.

This is the information age. Information is all around you, it is ready and easily available; you simply need to discover where to look and tap into all of the knowledge that can assist you on your journey. Your 'who' may not necessarily come in the form of face to face mentorship or a one to one with the gurus and specialists in your specified area. More often than not, your mentor will consist of several people through a plethora of resources such as forums, online web seminars, books, newsletters etc.

When I decided that I wanted to create lasting wealth I needed to find people who had successfully provided a home for their family, helped communities and touched other peoples' lives in a positive way. I knew I had to look for the right 'who'; people who had achieved the success that I aspired to. I needed to associate with those who have walked the talk rather than a high street financial adviser simply looking for their next commission.

I approached one of my colleagues that had about a dozen properties and was still working a 9-to-5. I invited her to lunch, asked questions and sought advice. But I did not stop there. I also did my own research, attended seminars and checked out forums with likeminded people. I joined the National Association of Landlords locally, nationally and internationally, which helped me stay current and keep abreast of changes. I bought and read books written by other agents and landlords who had created sustainable wealth in real estate.

WHO?
Chapter Four

I recently read a *Wealth Watch* newsletter where one of the UK's leading inheritance tax mitigation specialist's, James Bland, commented that when he advises people, he takes the view that they already know the reason why they have come to him. They simply need someone who can advise them on what to do to put the right structure in place before it is required. Bland stated that because there is not a 'one size fits all' solution, he bases his advice on the nature of the assets held in that family and how they want to control the way their assets are passed on to their love ones when they die. He said that when you do not know what to do you need someone to walk you through the alligator traps, as we live in an imperfect, infinite and complex world. Ignorance is expensive. Ensuring that you have the right 'who' will help when it comes to avoiding unnecessary pitfalls and steer you clear of the usual mistakes.

Questions for reflection

Complete the following questions and then review and reflect on your answers.

- Review your answers from the last two chapters and note down anything that stands out to you.

_____
_____
_____
_____

- Have any of your 'why' answers changed? If so, note down which ones.

  _____
  _____
  _____
  _____

- Why have your 'why' answers changed / stayed the same?

  _____
  _____
  _____
  _____

- Note down who or what is your 'who' and the reasons why.

  _____
  _____
  _____
  _____

Chapter Five
What?

When answering the 'what' question, action is required. Your 'what' answers will always require you to 'do' something.

Once you have resolved the 'why' question, decided on your 'who' (I call them 'divine helpers') and put them in your boat to sail; you are on your way. The next step is 'what' you need to do to achieve your objectives. You may have a mentor to guide you every step of the way or educational material to use. Once I resolved my 'why' and decided on my 'who', I drew up a plan that identified my 'what'.

While a burning desire is essential in order to achieve a dream, the other required ingredient is know-how; both are necessary for creating wealth. Every creation requires the correct tools for design and production. Not only will you require the right tools, you will also need the relevant knowledge. Your necessary tools may take shape in the form of habits, finances, skills, knowledge, relationship building etc.

Answer the questions below honestly:

What drives you?

_____

_____

_____

What principles guide your decisions?

_____

_____

_____

What do you ultimately want to achieve with your God-given life?

_____

_____

_____

What is your vision for the future?

_____

_____

_____

WHAT?
Chapter Five

Answering the questions above will help you locate your purpose. Once you are able to identify your purpose you will be able to obtain a roadmap for your life as well as reap spiritual and financial rewards.

So what else will you need to create your wealth? This depends on your 'why'.

Generally, you will need:

- *Funding* - capital or OPM (Other People's Money e.g. a bank loan or financial assistance provided by others including family and friends)
- *Effort*
- *Knowledge and Information*
- *Skills/Techniques/Education*
- *Time*
- *Discipline*
- *Focus*
- *Action*

Mix them all together, consistently and diligently and it will equal wealth.

We know that financial wealth is financial increase; another way to look at it is to say that you must increase your net worth financially by increasing your income and reducing your liabilities.

Now, I must add this point; borrowing money is not a sin. If you desire to start your wealth journey in real estate but need to borrow the capital to do so then that is up to you. Simply ensure that you make an informed decision and do not borrow at extortionate interest and repayment rates. What I desire to stress is that even if you start out this way, as I did, you must not plan to stay there. Take responsibility and save what you can. Aim to get to the place where you can buy and invest in property outright. Remember sole ownership is true ownership.

How do you get your income?

_____
_____
_____
_____

In his book *Rich Dad, Poor Dad;* Robert Kiyosaki states that there are three kinds of income categories:

1. *Earned income* – This is the most common type of income. It is earned from a job and is usually highly taxed, making it the most difficult to build wealth from. Earned income means working for somebody else and these days, no job is secure.

2. *Portfolio income* – This is income derived from paper assets or capital gains. Again, these are fairly common and easy to manage and maintain.

3. *Passive income* – This is income that comes in on a regular basis most commonly from real estate investments. It is more real

WHAT?
Chapter Five

in a sense as it is tangible. It should be noted that this type of income can also come from royalties and patents; there are tax advantages too.

However, I like to say there are 2 types of income. (1) The type you earn or exchange your time for and (2) The type you exchange your knowledge for. Most of us usually start with earned income; there is nothing wrong with starting in this way as long as you do not remain there. In my case, I worked 9 to 5 on most days and took on other part time jobs whilst studying. Eventually, I qualified as a mortgage broker and arranging mortgages for clients on a part time basis earned me much needed commission. The multiple income streams ensured that I met my savings target and acquired the capital I needed to start investing in real estate.

In effect, I converted my earned income into portfolio income or passive income. I moved from being a poor average monthly earner to comfortable, then to a state of wealth where my assets began to work for me.

My advice to those starting out based on my own experience is this:

- Ensure you manage your earned income effectively. Endeavour to save from any income you make, no matter how small it may seem because the pennies really do make the pounds. Use your time and skills to develop other potential sources of income so that you are eventually able to move to a wealthy state.

- Ensure you get the skills and abilities required to invest in your chosen vehicle (e.g. real estate). By educating yourself and reviewing ways of keeping abreast of changes, you can mitigate some investment risks.

One of the essential requirements to creating multiple income streams is education. The biggest reason a significant number of people fail in their goal to create lasting wealth is that they immediately begin to search for what they think they have to do to create wealth without asking 'why' first. An answer to this question would have led to 'who' is best placed to help, guide and mentor them to their destination of wealth creation. Instead they think "I need to make money, I'll go and see how others are making it so I can do the same." In my experience asking 'what' without the 'why' and 'who' will more often than not result in a waste of time, resources, money and effort.

A mentor or the 'who' may assist with guidance or advice on what may be required in terms of finance, skills etc. I was fortunate to have a friend who was already in real estate and owned some properties. Subsequent to his advice and guidance as well as the efforts I had made in educating myself on the subject, I decided that real estate was the right vehicle that would produce the kind of wealth I wanted to create. I knew real estate had the potential to be a long-term investment that appreciates in value and that I could pass it on to my family. Regardless of the recent crisis, real estate is still a good, long-term investment. Property is an 'inflation-proof' asset. If you look back over the last 30 years, real estate is still valued much higher than it was. And if you have tenants paying your mortgage, it can make the investment that much more profitable.

Questions for reflection

Complete the following questions and then review and reflect on your answers.

- What steps do you need to take to begin your wealth creation journey?

  _____
  _____
  _____
  _____

- What are your current obstacles and how can you overcome them?

  _____
  _____
  _____
  _____

- What do you envisage will be your biggest obstacles and how can you overcome or avoid them?

  _____
  _____
  _____
  _____

THE 5 W'S OF WEALTH CREATION
Keys to lasting wealth

Chapter Six
Financial Habits and Housekeeping

If you want to create wealth, you must cultivate the habits of a wealth creator. Discipline is an important habit that must be developed. Not only must you save; you must also plan what you will do with your savings to increase your potential for generating multiple streams of income. There must be a gradual move from physically working for a living to making your assets work for you. You must increase your earning potential and decrease your liabilities, which means you must spend less than you earn.

There is a myth out there that says you do not need to work harder just work smarter. This is a lie because it is only a partial truth. In order to succeed you must work harder but you must also work smarter. One can never replace the other. Working hard is just as important as working smart! Don't be afraid of hard work, there is profit in labour. [8] Be prepared to roll your sleeves up and get stuck in. This is partly why choosing to do something you are passionate about and have great interest in is vital.

To increase your worth:

- Take stock of all your income - right down to the nearest penny.

- Prioritise your outgoings. Start with the most essential, then prioritise debts, bills and where possible, arrange an automated process to pay them via direct debit or standing order. Your outgoings should not be more than 30/40% of your total income.

- Make about 5% of your income readily available for emergencies in an easy to access account.

- Save a minimum of 15% from all income via an automated system in a high interest notice account so that a penalty is incurred should money be withdrawn without the agreed notice period given. Remember this is your 'seed to acquire assets'.

To create lasting wealth a personal finance ladder should then be followed in this order.

You cannot be truly wealthy and owe money so if you are currently in debt, a debt free plan should be your priority. You could start by opening a separate bank account and naming it the 'debt reduction account'. All of the money in the account can go towards reducing debts. Set up a standing order from this account to reduce your debts until they are all paid off. Ensure high interest loan installments or liabilities are paid off first. Liabilities may include rent or mortgage payments, insurance, electricity and gas bills etc.

Save excess income by automation. "I don't have any excess income!" I hear you say. Well what about your daily routine and habits? You would be surprised how much extra savings can be accrued.

- Get rid of bad habits. (i.e. spending all your 'loose change' on smoking. If you quit smoking, you could save an average of £26.00 per week. Invest this amount in a pension pot for 30 years and it will yield £116,000.00.)

- Switch home loans or credit cards to those with better deals by comparing rates.

- Cancel subscription television such as SKY TV and opt for Free View or pay as you go television.

- Cut back on coffee shop coffees; make your own as well as your own packed lunches. A £3.00 sandwich five days a week adds up to a big expense annually.

- Save pay rises. Do not live by Parkinson's Law of economics that says expenses will always rise with income. While this may be generally true, you can discipline yourself. Don't spend tomorrow's prosperity today. If you are currently on a chicken budget then do not buy steak! If a steak pay slip comes don't spend it all. Keep living on the chicken budget and watch your savings increase!

- Go for cheaper car insurance cover, phone contracts and broadband. If you purchase them online, use a cash back website.

- Do not register with expensive gyms if you do not use them regularly. Go for a run in the park or invest in a treadmill instead.

- Create a Budget, including all bills and expenses, and stick to it.
- Avoid carrying cash, it can be harder to account for.
- Use your debit card to pay for things and if you owe money on your credit cards leave them at home or cut them up!

Savings Ladder

- Make use and take advantage of tax-free savings.
- If you have employer contribution assistance make use of it for your pension.
- Open an investment savings account. (i.e. Deliberately put away all your extra savings for acquisition of future assets)

Investors' Habits

In my experience, there are two reasons given by most of those who fail to achieve financial freedom or set up their own businesses; FEAR AND FINANCES. The fear of losing the money invested and fear of the business failing. The fear of loss is weightier than the desire to gain or the freedom and flexibility that come with owning a business. With a family, mortgage and all the responsibility that comes with these things, it may be deemed foolish or even reckless to risk starting a business. As a result, many refuse to jeopardise their 'safe and secure' 9-5 job. I call it the preference to be a 'slave to the wage slip'. Many are bound by a false sense of security – yes the bills may be paid and a certain guaranteed amount may be deposited into your account monthly but there is no real 'security' when working for someone else. Jobs are lost every single day and what's more the earning potential is capped.

Despite being afraid, a wealth creator will take the leap and do it anyway. They will take the risk because it is worth it. He or she will not let fear stop them from crossing over from wage earner to wealth creator.

Lack of finance should never be used as an excuse to do nothing. A budding wealth creator should use their initiative to think about other avenues of finance (i.e. banks, sponsors, loans or other people's money).

Other people's money may be used to invest in real estate. Just ensure that you have made some contribution towards the deposit to get a better deal and put aside some funds to meet your responsibilities as a landlord. I shall discuss this in detail in a later chapter.

In conclusion, the financial habit or main goal of an investor should be to create an investment portfolio that produces passive income, giving the investor the flexibility and freedom to choose how to spend their time and money.

Investor habits should include striving to increase worth:

1. Plant your own money tree that will keep growing residual money year after year. The catalyst could be a business, product, service or assets that continue to provide money even after you have stopped working.

2. You must endeavour to develop multiple streams of income. When you are trying to save to purchase assets that increase in value, you must look in to multiple income streams. I believe being self-employed or having your own business creates this route.

Benefits of owning your own business

There is no limit to what you can earn once you are self-employed or run your own business. However, there is a limit to what you can earn when employed. It has been said that "the rich own businesses and the poor work for them".

No matter how big the salary an employee earns or has the capacity to earn, unless they invest in assets that can produce income, it will not last. The salary may be high if they continue to work for that organisation but market changes or retirement may ultimately affect earnings. However if you have your own thriving business, then you can continue to earn for a very long time.

One of the disadvantages of being an employee is the constraint in terms of time. There is also the added problem of lack of job security. Owning your business provides the flexibility to plan your time around your priorities and what you value most. This could be spending more time with your family or even devoting more time to playing golf!

Questions for reflection

Complete the following questions and then review and reflect on your answers.

- List your current source(s) of income.

_____

_____

_____

_____

- How could you increase your savings?

  _____
  _____
  _____
  _____

- List five plausible ideas that could generate more income.

  _____
  _____
  _____
  _____

- Do you have any expensive, or costly habits? (e.g. buying coffee every day before work, getting a weekly pedicure or manicure) If so, calculate how much it is costing you per annum and find a way to reduce the cost.

  _____
  _____
  _____
  _____

THE 5 W'S OF WEALTH CREATION
Keys to lasting wealth

Chapter Seven
How do I get there?

The terms "vehicle of wealth creation" and "pillars of wealth" refer to the route or routes a person chooses to take to create their wealth. If wealth creation is akin to a journey; what is the most suitable vehicle required to take the wealth creator to his or her destination?

The questions you must ask *before* committing to a purchase are similar to buying any product; what are the benefits? Does it satisfy my needs? Can I afford it? Is it value for money? When it comes to investment you must take the questioning one step further and ask "can I maintain, monitor and add value to the investment?"

The vehicle or pillars of wealth can be divided into three main categories:

1. Building a business
2. Investing in the stock market
3. Investing in real estate

Each of the categories listed above, if invested correctly and handled wisely, can create wealth.

So, why would you choose to invest in one over the other? Why not invest in all three?

No category is better than the other. Now, it is possible to argue that one category may have less risk than another or even produce a greater return at a faster rate but the key is this: You must choose the category that best suits you and furnishes your ideas and concepts. You must be passionate about whatever you choose.

Dolf de Roos, a successful real estate investor, made this quote: "The rich either made their wealth, or kept their wealth, in real estate". However you choose to embark upon your journey of wealth creation; the likelihood is that, if successful, real estate will become part of your portfolio.

My choice and my reasons:

I chose real estate and so that is what I will place emphasis on, as I have done throughout the booklet.

I believe that real estate investment is the most beneficial of all the options. When done correctly, it provides income, capital appreciation and can appreciate in value over time.

Personally, real estate offered me the means of building substantial long-term wealth in a safe, stable and predictable manner. It is almost impossible to lose 100% of property value in comparison to the stock market where the value of shares and stocks can literally be wiped out overnight.

History has shown that property, as an investment, doubles in value every eight years. [9] Investing in property is a long term wealth building strategy and as such, short term fluctuations in property prices have little impact on the investments ability to generate strong returns over time.

Leverage or gearing as it is often called, is one of the major attractions of investing in property. An investor can generate a high return on the capital invested through borrowed money simply because it is easy to borrow most of a property's value. Therefore very small sums of personal investment are required to begin building your property portfolio. Because of this, the return on capital through property investment can be far higher that through other investment routes. Personally, I cannot think of any other form of investment, which offers the potential for huge returns with a small cash outlay to create wealth that lasts.

Benefits of real estate investment:

- Long term, it is an appreciating asset.

- If you invest well, your tenants will pay most of or more than the cost of ownership and maintenance.

- You can borrow most of the purchase price.

Can I afford it?

If you do not have all the funds required, you can usually obtain a bank loan. This is unlike other avenues of wealth creation where banks are not readily willing to lend (e.g. stocks and shares or a 'risky' start-up business).

I could not afford to buy my first piece of real estate in cash. I used other funds that were available to me at the time. My savings, a £5,000.00 unsecured loan and interest free credit card cheques all added up and I was able to put down a deposit for a £55,000 flat. I then let it out for £600.00 per month (i.e. an 8/9% yield).

In real estate even if you cannot afford it, there are lenders, and in some cases family members, who will be happy to assist if you have a good record of financial management or if there is an element of trust.

Can I manage, monitor or add value to real estate so that its value increases?

Property is a tangible asset that you own and control. Because of this you can impact its ability to perform through simple measures such as decorating or adding space. By furnishing the property it is possible to not only increase the rental income but also determine the kind of tenant you will attract. The tenant will pay you rent which will ideally cover the costs of financing, maintaining and managing your property investment. Compare this to the stock market where you have limited control over what can happen to your investment. You cannot directly influence decisions made on a company's choice of direction and as such, the performance of your investment is very much under someone else's control. So, with an appreciating asset bought with someone else's money and maintained by monthly income from your tenant, why wouldn't you want to invest in property?

If you choose real estate as your vehicle both to achieve financial freedom and develop a passive income or save towards a comfortable retirement, as an investor there are some fundamental questions that need to be answered.

'Must answer' questions before a potential real estate investor proceeds:

Type of property to buy – This is one of the most important decisions a potential real estate investor will make. The answer will depend on why real estate was chosen as the appropriate vehicle. Was it chosen as a means to provide income, capital appreciation or both? Each of the property types listed below has advantages, depending on the investor's plans and experience.

Houses / Single-family dwelling / Flats / Mid terraced / Detached / Semi-detached / Mobiles homes / Conversions /Apartment buildings / Student accommodation / Commercial property / Development.

The choice you make as an investor will determine the type of tenant that will inhabit your property.

Type of approach – Buy and hold (buy-to-let) / trading (i.e. where you buy at a discount and resell within months - mostly on off plan) / Renovations (i.e. buy, refurbish and sell on) / Foreclosures.

The type of approach chosen will depend on your goals and circumstances from the beginning of your journey.

Awareness of landlord responsibility:

A potential investor landlord who wants to be successful with their wealth creation must be prepared to take the necessary time and effort to ask about the relevant key responsibilities of taking on such a role before making an investment decision.

Whether you become a landlord by choice or default, (i.e. you are unable to sell your property but need to move, you inherited a property or you set out to buy one) you must be aware that a landlord has significant responsibilities. Indeed some landlords that I have met forget that they are running a business. Property ownership should never be treated as such. From the day the keys are handed over to the tenant, you are running a business and must be aware of the relevant legal obligations, tests, inspection requirements and financial responsibilities required. You must also be up to speed with the increasing local licensing schemes in the area.

How to be an effective landlord:

Apart from the business elements of what makes a successful property investor/landlord, there are other mandatory requirements:

Communication – To manage property efficiently, a landlord has to be a good communicator and must be able to deal with a variety of people across the real estate profession (e.g., letting agents and tenants).

Property Etiquette – An effective landlord is proactive - keeping the property in good condition at all times. They have the ability to resolve issues and can always add a personal touch, like sending Christmas cards or a 'welcome to your new home' note to tenants. It may sound insignificant but small things like this will help foster good working relationships.

Financial Prowess – Financial astuteness is a key requirement. Financial reserves must be made available to deal with emergencies, unforeseen problems, repairs and breakdown of appliances as well as anything else the landlord is responsible for. Time is money and so a successful landlord ensures that time is factored in to undertake regular or routine inspections of the property.

Record Keeping – Records of receipts, gas / electric certificates, inspection reports and all documents related to the property must be kept for deposit protection, tax and other purposes. There have been known instances where legal cases have been lost due to the landlord's inability to provide the required information or documentation.

The 'buy-to-let' vehicle is different from the other forms of investments. A variety of disciplines and a hands-on approach is required to make it a successful venture. Thorough research into potential returns of the existing market as well as the impact of interest rate rises, legislative changes and local schemes, such as a mandatory licensing scheme, must be carried out.

When and where can I invest in real estate?

Timing is important; it is akin to raising children. They are guided through what is right and wrong from the early years and are expected to know the difference once they are of age. A similar principle applies to real estate investment. Understanding right and wrong investment is crucial. The purchase of property can be done at various times to take advantage of the market position – it depends on what you are looking for. What is wrong for you and your specific requirements may be right for someone else. Professional property investors however, tend to buy when property is cheaper as money is made when the property is bought and not when it is sold. Profit can also be released when prices are rising and the decision is made to sell. The key is understanding the market and having a clear picture of the climate when you buy. There is no wrong or right time specifically, but wrong investments can be made if essential research is not conducted first.

The popular saying: "Location, location, location" in relation to where a prospective property buyer decides to buy cannot be underestimated. Location is critical as it can determine the wealth potential.

If the chosen vehicle of wealth creation is the stock market, the investor would have undertaken the appropriate research required to ensure that their stocks and shares were chosen from companies that would perform. In the same way the secret of making significant money from property, is to buy properties which will outperform the market and not just follow it. This is where location can play a vital role.

We all know that these days, there are quite a significant number of accidental buy-to-let landlords. There are those who buy property regardless of the location and just wait for the value to appreciate before selling it, moving on and then doing the same elsewhere. This is known as 'flipping' and it is a short-term measure. The fact is, in a property market where the long-term trend is upwards - any property, regardless of its condition, will increase in value at some point. However, the best opportunities to outperform within the property market is through buying in the right location.

This logic applies to property investment internationally. Gulf news reported in April 2014, that billionaires see a safe haven in real estate especially in locations where demand and pay are high. London topped the list of these premier locations; Singapore and Mumbai also saw a record jump of 45% to 166% increase and it was noted that property value in Dubai was also on the rise.

An experienced real estate investor will look for up and coming areas and then look at the areas adjacent to places that are already popular. Nearby areas usually benefit from the 'ripple effect' - where buyers who cannot afford a prime area compromise on location and buy a home in a neighbouring postcode. Even in London there are postcodes which represent fantastic value when compared to the more affluent postcodes that surround them. Areas with good transport connections and local amenities, which have benefited from substantial government regeneration funds are also good potentials. Property prices will usually surge ahead in these locations, as the desirability of the area improves. Sometimes the benefits may take time to materialise initially due to poor transportation infrastructure, however, history shows that over time, these locations prove to be the best investments.

A typical example that I experienced was in the London Docklands/ Thames Gateway area which benefited from a considerable government regeneration programme in the 1980s. It took many years to establish the Docklands as a desirable area to live in. However, during the 1990s as the transport infrastructure improved and a few more local amenities came on stream, the Docklands began to really take off and is now firmly established as a new regeneration scheme.

Questions for reflection

Complete the following questions and then review and reflect on your answers.

- Review the three vehicles of wealth creation categories. Identify the one that best suits you and why.

_____
_____
_____
_____

- What are the key ingredients required to make an effective landlord?

_____
_____
_____
_____

- What type(s) of property do you desire to buy and why?

_____
_____
_____
_____

- Identify four up and coming locations. List what would make each area a good investment and why.

_____
_____
_____
_____

THE 5 W'S OF WEALTH CREATION

Keys to lasting wealth

Chapter Eight
Nuggets of Wealth Creation

The nuggets below are little gems of truth with valuable facts and ideas that will propel you into wealth creation and sustain you during your journey.

A

Attitude

Everybody has an attitude. A negative attitude is destructive and unsettling, whilst a positive attitude is affirming and constructive. Attitude is a choice. You may not always be able to control what happens in your life but you can always control how you react!

Having a positive outlook does not mean that everything in your life will be perfect. It does mean accepting, hoping and working toward a good result in every situation that comes your way. Christians call it hope, it is the substance of their faith - all things work together for good for those who love God [10] Develop a positive attitude toward your course of creating wealth. Use your creative energy to find ways things can be achieved or created, instead of exhausting your mental and emotional vitality on dead ends. Having a positive attitude means you focus on the things you want to happen; refusing to throw your toys out of the pram when things go wrong or the results are contrary to your expectations. Use positive affirmations. Yes be realistic, but choose to see the glass half full and strategise on how to fill the other half!

You must have a positive outlook of things, always looking for a solution; as your attitude determines your altitude.

Accountability

Wealth creators must be accountable and always take responsibility for their actions. Being critical and judgmental when things go wrong will never solve the problem. Instead of playing the blame game, turn the situation into a lessons learned exercise and use your efforts to correct things. Always keep your destination, the end goal, in sight.

Action

Yes you need a dream, but simply having a dream is not enough. A wealth creator does not just dream; a wealth creator will invest in their dream. Be diligent in your course of work and what you believe in – take action and live out your dream. Most people fail not because their idea is poor but because they either do nothing with it or give up easily. You must take the necessary action required to go to the next stage.

First time winners are rare, but success will come if you do not give up. Persist until it happens! Success is never a walk in the park. It takes effort, hard work, smart work, time, finances, endurance, skill and ability.

B

Believe

Your belief is closely linked to your confidence. It is your conviction in your ability to achieve what you set out to do. You must have the belief that anything is possible.

Do you believe in yourself and your capability? Do you believe in your 'why'?

Behaviour

In your journey to wealth creation, you will need to have winning behaviour that mirrors your positive attitude. This means you stay motivated at all times and do not allow setbacks to deviate you from your goal; you will soon see that your mind will follow.

Budget

A wealth creator must budget and avoid waste. Unexpected costs may arise but a good budget will build in a contingency and ensure that you do not spend unnecessarily. Having a budget will also help you think and plan for unforeseen costs.

C

Creativity

The world is full of products created by individuals who dared to think outside the ordinary and ask creative questions. Their creativity contributes to the services and products that make the world a better, more efficient and innovative place. Successful entrepreneurs who have created products or services that are in demand have done so by removing every limitation. They have faced the impossible and realised their dream.

Confidence

Confidence comes from 'know how'. A confident person is skilful in what they do, knows what they are talking about and keeps abreast of changes through education and on-going learning (i.e. through networking/social clubs/mentors etc.).

In her book *The Confident Woman*, Joyce Meyer stated that having confidence in what we can do and not worrying about anything else is like stepping out of the boat and into the water! Will you take a leap of confidence and dare to step out?

Communication

Without the ability to communicate effectively with others, some entrepreneurs have lost considerable opportunities to make money. You must communicate well with your team, tenants, mentors and all others involved. Remember – effective communication is as much about listening as it is about getting your point across.

Courage

Courage is a very special quality — and some would say that it is becoming increasingly rare. The ancient Greeks held courage to be the foundational trait of all other virtues. What is the difference between an average leader and a great leader? What separates an average parent and an outstanding one? The difference is courage.

Courage is often understood to have two categories: physical and moral. Physical courage is the willingness to face serious risk to life or limb. Moral courage is the firmness of mind, will and emotion and the conviction of right and wrong that faces the dilemma, danger or difficulty without flinching or retreating. The American Civil War General, William T. Sherman, understood courage. He said, "Courage is awareness of the true measure of danger, and the mental willingness to endure it." John Wayne put it more simply: "Courage is being scared to death and saddling up anyway."

A lack of courage is what makes some people crack under pressure, whether in warfare or business, while those with courage seem to push past their limits. As Audrey Hepburn said, "Nothing is impossible, the word itself says I'm possible!"

It takes courage to handle criticism and withstand it, it takes courage to act even though you have doubt. Without courage, most will never step out on to the journey of wealth building, depriving themselves and settling for temporary pleasure and short term gain. Courage is saying no to wasteful material pleasure.

Courage has been the mark of outstanding men and women throughout history confronted with the same choices. Some accepted the challenge, while others shrunk away. Wealth creators must have the courage to face failure and use it as a stepping stone to learn and improve. It takes courage to begin again on any failed project, especially if all is against you.

Commitment

You must be willing, devoted and dedicated to the available resources, energy, time and money and place all efforts into creating wealth. Wealth is a process, it is a marathon – not a sprint. Without commitment many goals and visions are not accomplished.

Current

It has been said that being current is the currency of life. This means not just keeping current but being flexible and open to change or learn new things in order to reach your destination. Change is a constant that we have in life – it is guaranteed, so it's important that you continue to keep abreast of change as it happens. Change *with* the change or change *ahead* of the change but never change behind it.

Counting Costs

Are you willing to pay the price? Before a building is built a blueprint is created and a budget is drawn up to ensure that the expenses are monitored and the building is finished. Do you know what wealth creation will cost you? The price is different for everyone; for some it is the price of delayed gratification, for others it is investing time and energy into research, and understanding.

Whatever the case you must count the cost. Every creation will involve the exchange of something, either in monetary terms, time or relationship. You must factor the mental, physical, social, and emotional, as well as financial, costs and plan them into your wealth creation journey.

Character

"Character is like a tree and reputation is like its shadow. The shadow is what we think of it; the tree is the real thing." - Abraham Lincoln

Your character is who you really are and it will proceed you long after you have left this earth. A wealth creator must be able develop the character of a winner and should always have a futuristic outlook coupled with integrity.

D

Dream

A person can only reach their destination if they have an idea of where they are going. A wealth creator must have a dream, a mental picture of where he or she is going. There must be a purpose or a defined destination. As the saying goes; "a man without a purpose or a sense of where he is going will die a commoner".

Desire

A dream without the desire to bring it to pass will eventually die. Desire creates the necessary fuel and passion that is required to make things happen.

"Desire is the starting point of all achievement, not a hope, not a wish, but a keen pulsating desire which transcends everything." — Napoleon Hill: Early pioneer of personal success literature; author of *Think and Grow Rich*.

Discipline

The core areas a wealth investor must focus on the most, are what I call the 3 disciplines:

1. *Discipline of mindset* - Do not let negative or trivial thoughts into your mind. Be disciplined about what information you allow in. Set your mind on beneficial thoughts by focusing on positive information. This will enhance your capability for creativity.

2. *Discipline of relationships* – The old proverb "Show me your friends and I will show you who you are" rings true. Who are you acquainted with? Who are you networking with? Who do you brainstorm with? Those you choose to spend your time with will influence the way you perceive, the way you are perceived and the decisions you make.

3. *Discipline of management (money/time /opportunities)* - This is all about focusing on the end goal. You must use opportunities, money and time effectively - through good management.

One of the ways I disciplined myself, when it came to saving, was to ensure every penny of income I had was accounted for. Through discipline, my savings were made via direct debit or standing order to the tune of 15% of my income.

Determination

I believe a person with a dream, who is diligent and determined will arrive at their destination no matter what obstacles they may encounter.

As the ruler of Dubai UAE, Sheikh Mohamed bin Rashid al Martin met 36 young investors at the Dubai International Financial Centre in April 2014 and said, *"Dubai is a model for overcoming the consequences of the global financial crisis by determination, planning, realistic vision and serious work."*

If there is no determination then there will be no drive to thrust forwards.

E

Education

When I use the word education, I am specifically referring to knowledge and information about financial wealth - especially the vehicle you have chosen to make your wealth. Do you know the mechanics of money? Do you know the various bank accounts out there that prove beneficial for your cause? What do you know about taxation? Educating yourself in these matters is important, as there is nothing worse than making money yet being unable to keep it or increase it.

Enthusiasm

Get excited about the vehicle you have chosen to create your wealth. Become enthusiastic about the journey you have decided to embark upon and the outcomes you seek. Your energy and enthusiasm will help you succeed even if others do not share your excitement.

F

Faith

You need faith to create what you do not yet have. Faith gives a tangible form to hope. It is the brother of belief and leaves you with confidence and an enablement that your dreams, no matter how big, can be achieved.

Focus

If you aim at nothing, you will hit it every time. Focus provides the timely milestones that tell you achievement is on the horizon. Without focus there is no centre of interest or visual to pay attention to; distraction is commonplace and quitting becomes second nature.

Flexibility

Markets change, processes change and people change. Nothing stays the same. You must be seamless, quick and flexible when adapting to change. You cannot afford to be rigid in your way of thinking, especially when there is always so much to learn.

G

Goals

A war is always won by the victory of many small and seemingly insignificant battles. Your vision is your ultimate destination and goals are the stepping blocks that will get you there. Having a goal is like having a road map to get you to your destination. It is important that you have short-term and long-term goals. They provide a catalyst for motivation at every stage of the journey.

Defined short-term (small) goals are beneficial as they highlight reaching small milestones and often give a rush of energy and excitement, which can keep you going until you reach the finish line. Long-term (large) goals can take more time to accomplish but will always create a point of focus.

Be sure to write down your short-term and long-term goals and place them in front of you daily. Save them on your phone, computer or anywhere you can read them daily. [11] Setting daily, weekly, monthly or yearly goals is good practice. They will guide you through to your desired destination and can act as checklists or reference points to ensure you remain focused and on track.

I set my daily goals and place them in front of my personal computer, on the office wall, in my bedroom and even in my rest room! There are no excuses because I continually keep them before my eyes. Each small victory I achieve takes me one step closer towards winning the war and realising my vision.

K

Knowledge

Knowledge is power and it is the application of knowledge that produces the desired results.

Did you know that if you invested just £5,000 per year at an average return of 7% from the age of 25 you would be a millionaire by the time you reached 65 through compound interest? The pennies do make the pounds. If you decide on an amount you are able to save each month, and stick with it, you will see your money grow.

L

Listen and learn

Wealth creators are both learners and listeners.

To be successful you must be willing to learn and listen. I am sure you have heard of others people's knowledge or OPK. These are mentors, or those who have already been to where you are going. I often read reviews by those who have used products I desire to buy; they usually help me make an informed choice. Having a mentor can work in the same way.

Ignorance is not wrong. We are all ignorant in one area or another; no one knows it all. Realising your ignorance and choosing to do nothing about it is not only foolish but costly. Try to learn a new thing daily, especially where finance and wealth creation are concerned. Improve your areas of weakness by focusing on sharpening your skills and building good character. Listen to and learn from other people.

Leverage

One of the most common reasons given by people as to why they cannot attain financial freedom or create the wealth they desire is that they do not have money. That does not need to be the case, you can leverage and use other people's money responsibly.

M

Mindset

This is one of the most important factors for anyone who wants to create financial wealth because battles are either won or lost in the mind.

Whatever you think about, you eventually become. A mind shift is required to create true wealth. The mindset of an entrepreneur is the most important factor in creating financial wealth. You must replace the belief that not everyone has ability to create wealth with a mindset that understands everyone holds the seed of creativity and the ability to achieve success within them. Stop thinking about working for money and start thinking about how you can make money work for you. Remove any disempowering beliefs you have about yourself or money.

Motivation

Wealth creation is a journey that includes ups and downs. Unless you are motivated by your 'why', you will give up in the middle of the journey. It is true that the best antidote to discouragement is motivation. A motivated person does not give up easily.

You are the only one who can take responsibility for making certain that you stay motivated no matter the circumstances. Others may try to motivate you for a short term, (e.g. via seminars) however this can be short lived and almost non-existent once you face chaos during your journey. The reality is you spend more time with yourself than anyone else, so it is most logical to take the time to motivate yourself.

In his book, *How to be Motivated all the Time*, PJ Daniels comments that motivation is a personal thing. It can be learned and become a lifestyle. It is a disciplined personality that creates a new relationship and only you can act it out. This means to reverse all negativity and become optimistic, positive, confident, objective and successful about your cause. [12]

Managing

You will eventually lose the things in life that you mismanage or fail to value. A wealth creator must be able to manage, maximise and multiply all resources that come into his/her hands; this includes relationships, time and opportunities.

Every penny that comes into your hands is a seed to create something with. Maturity is the ability to successfully manage which seeds are for eating and which are for sowing. Creating wealth is not only about making money but making every penny count and avoiding waste at all costs. Ensure that you are not only able to make money but also able to keep some back to invest and create your tree of wealth.

Monitoring

Debt has become so commonplace today that most people do not know whether they are coming or going. Keeping your head above water and scraping by from month to month, whilst your feet paddle frantically to stop you drowning, is evidence of poor monitoring. Do you keep note of what you earn, save and spend? Do you know when your account is overdrawn and what type of interest you are being charged? Make sure that you observe, check and keep continuous records of your affairs. If you know what's going on with your finances then you are less likely to be hit with any nasty surprises down the line.

Mitigate against risks

Plan out strategies for potential problems. Setbacks and obstacles are inevitable for a wealth creator. They must be expected and mitigated against. A buy-to-let investor will know that having the type of insurance that covers the building, repairs and rent is wise. It will aid in avoiding the risk of negative accounts or even losing your investment completely. Are you reviewing your accounts regularly and taking advantage of the best products available?

O

Organisation

Without organisation, time and financial resources will go down the drain of wastage. To be successful in any profession or business you must be organised. This consists of:

Physical organisation: have a system to organise documents, files, schedules etc.

Mental organisation: prioritise and be prepared for any eventuality.

P

Purpose

Without a purpose for creating something, whatever is created will result in wastage as the benefit of its creation will be meaningless.

Purpose is one of those subjects most of us avoid but we all want the answer to. It's a question everyone asks, "What am I here for?" Your purpose is part of your makeup, it is engrained in who you were created to be. Having purpose is what will provide you with a 'why' answer that endures.

Passion

Passion for your purpose will create prosperity. Whatever you are passionate about, you create. Your passion for wanting to create a thing reflects your belief of why you need that thing to be created. Without passion, a purpose cannot be realised.

Richard Branson, expressed that one of the most important ingredients of a successful entrepreneur or a visionary is passion. Whatever you want out of life – become passionate about it.

Priorities

Without setting priorities, all efforts become fruitless. A man without a target to hit will hit at anything that comes. People of principle achieve targets because people of principle are people with priorities.

Planning

Wealth creation is a journey and every journey requires a plan. You should map out a plan and timeline that will lead you to your destination.

Preparation

Rain is of no use to a farmer without seed in the ground - he will have nothing to harvest. Even with the right opportunities and mentors, a plan can fail without adequate preparation. You can plan a journey but unless you prepare for it, the plan will fail. Preparation coupled with opportunity produces productivity and success.

S

Start

You cannot dream forever or plan for ever. At some point, you will need to start the work. Success is unattainable without a start. If someone wants a new body, they must get up, start moving and start eating better. What are you waiting for? Make that call, ask that question, change your 'I don't know' by finding someone who does. Start. The worst that can happen is you fail and that is a lesson on its own.

Succeed

I think Eric Thomas, the well know motivational speaker, put it best when he said; "When you want to succeed as bad as you want to breathe, then you will be successful."

T

Thought

There is something truly special about the power of thought. Think positive, wealth creating thoughts on your way to creating wealth.

Whatever you can conceive and believe, you will achieve. For instance, if you think about misfortune, you'll *expect* misfortune to happen and it will. Winners think about winning while losers think about losing.

Successful people think of themselves as successful.

At the first obstacle, a loser will say to himself "I never win anyway", this ensures he loses because he expects to. Whereas a winner who loses will say "this is just a small glitch. It's not a big deal" as a result, he continues his journey until he succeeds.

Time Management

To create wealth you must be able to understand timing and manage your time effectively.

Time is given to us all in the same measure. Each day 24 hours is given to both the rich and the poor. When it is lost or wasted it cannot be recovered. Time wasted is time lost.

There is a time to sow and a time to reap. Your time is not just a commodity; it is the priciest commodity known to mankind. Your time is your life. You and you alone are in control of your time and you must be able to plan ahead in order to make the most of the time available.

Wealth can be created at any time but discerning the correct season is pivotal. For example, there is a time to save and raise finance, if you plan to acquire assets. If you start early you will reap the benefits early. For example, saving on an ISA account is tax-efficient; to gain maximum allowance benefits each year you must save in the scheme at the beginning of each financial year. However, if you start later, you still reap benefits but they will be about 50% less than those who started on time.

This is also true of real estate investment. You can make money at any time in real estate, especially if you have range within your portfolio and you have positioned yourself well for the different cycles. If it is a sellers' market where prices are rising, with low supply of properties in the market, you can become a seller and take advantage of the cycle as you have purchased in an undervalued market at a time when property was cheap. If it is a buyer's market, also known as a fallen market, where there is more supply than demand, then you can purchase more property at a discount because you have the financial capability and are ready to take the appropriate action within the cycle. By doing this, you prepare for another cycle in the future to buy low and sell high. In real estate you make money when you buy (if bought at the right price i.e. undervalue or at a discount) and not when you sell.

Answer the following questions and then review and reflect on them.

- List what you believe to be the three most important traits from the wealth nuggets and explain why.

_____
_____
_____
_____

- What are the weakest areas of your character?

_____
_____
_____
_____

- How can you improve your weak areas?

_____

_____

_____

_____

Chapter Nine
Actions for Lasting Wealth

In this chapter, I will discuss essential yet simple daily actions required to help you to create lasting wealth.

Essential steps to wealth:

- *Develop a wealth mindset.* The reason why this is important is because no one can do it for you. You must believe within you that you have the ability and capability inside of you to be wealthy. Settle this 'why' question in your mind and all other actions will follow. This is the reason I emphasised the importance of asking yourself the question 'why' you want to be wealthy in previous chapters. If you are clear about 'why', then the planning of your journey will begin to fall in place.

- *Cultivate 'wealthy' behaviour.* You must spend less than you earn and save or invest the rest. Save from all available income to build up a deposit towards your investment. Your number one wealth-building tool is your income, but if you are in debt, that tool is broken and has to be mended before you can use it to create wealth.

If you are in debt, pay it off. You cannot be wealthy if creditors are pursuing you. Remember, if wealth is the residual of your total assets less your liability, then you cannot be wealthy if the total of the debt you owe is more than your assets.

How do I do this you ask? If you are in debt, follow the steps I have outlined below and start to reduce your debts. Take appropriate action now.

1. Take two sheets of paper and write down your outgoings in order of priority on the first sheet. By priority I mean in order of essentiality. So, rent/ mortgage first and then utilities (i.e. Gas / electricity). Highlight the debts that accrue the highest interest rate repayments.

2. Write down all income received on the second sheet.

3. Review all the debts noted and make changes so that those that attract the highest interest are paid off first. Try to allocate approximately 10% of your income towards these debts. Set up a standing order and a specific bank account so the money is deducted directly from your income and paid towards your outstanding debts.

4. Review your circumstances and make the necessary adjustments to minimise waste. Are you under occupying in your current property? How many times do you eat out weekly and will a

packed lunch make you some savings? How much do you spend on transportation and entertainment? Can you make any adjustments to reduce the related outgoings?

5. Educate yourself in learning the mechanics of money. Tool strategies and investment vehicles must all be learnt and understood if you are to use them to take you through your journey. Develop your understanding of banking mechanics (i.e. savings types, compound interest, types of assets - including paper assets, shares, bonds and pensions). Learn about the different types of real estate including residential, commercial and new build developments, as well as business start-ups and buying or franchising. You must also learn the language by familiarising yourself with the terminology used in investment.

6. Acquire appreciating assets with the savings or residual income you have built up and reduce your liabilities. Remember to create lasting long-term wealth you must acquire a portfolio of assets that generate income.

1 Q: Are you a wealth creator or just a wealth consumer?

Your answers to the questions below will give you a clue...

- *Do you love to spend and hate to save?*

- *Do you spend lots and save little?*

- *Do you you spend most or all of your income (SEED)?*

Are you a seed sower or seed eater? If you answered yes to any of the three questions above then...

A: This means you have the habit of a consumer and not an investor. You enjoy spending all income earned without saving towards acquiring assets that will generate income, no matter how small. If you want to create wealth, this will need to change.

2 Q: Do you believe in using your God-given ability, skills, opportunities and current finances to start; even if you are afraid you may fail?

A: If you are a nonstarter due to fear, then you have the habit of a consumer.

Chapter Ten
Work book

Below, you have a list of essential wealth creation questions to answer. Why don't you put them to the test? Take a moment and apply the principles of wealth creation.

Answer the following questions thoroughly. It might be a good idea to jot your answers in a notebook so that you can expand on them, conduct necessary research and amend when and where necessary.

- Why do you want to create wealth and which vehicle are you able to start with? (e.g. business/ real estate/paper assets)

_____
_____
_____
_____

- Who do you think can help you? (A mentor or products in the form of books, information, seminars, forums).

  _____
  _____
  _____
  _____

- What tools do you have to work with right now? (e.g. finance/savings, time, training)

  _____
  _____
  _____
  _____

- What tools do you need to obtain in order to achieve your goal and how can you access them? (e.g. education, training, finance skills, savings etc.)

  _____
  _____
  _____
  _____

- Where are you able to maximise your goal? Can it be in any location?

  _____
  _____
  _____
  _____

- When are you able to start? (list dates, timings and timeframes)

_____
_____
_____
_____

- What are your weaknesses and how can you improve them?

_____
_____
_____
_____

Once you have thoroughly answered all the questions above, then:

Plan ahead. Put activity and strategy into daily, weekly, monthly and yearly goals.

Prepare. You may need some training. You may also need to save, pay off some debts and tidy up your credit file.

Act. You must take action. Book that training course, make that call, arrange that appointment and view that house.

TAKE A STEP OF FAITH TOWARDS ACHIEVING YOUR DREAM TODAY. I believe when answered sincerely and followed dutifully, the above questions and steps identified in this book will help you on your journey to creating true, lasting wealth. Remember, financial freedom is possible and wealth creation is attainable; you simply need to ask the right questions, plan, prepare and then take action!

THE 5 W'S OF WEALTH CREATION
Keys to lasting wealth

FOOTNOTES

1. Marketing Mastery "Forbes 400 Best Way to Build Wealth" http://www.ourmarketingmastery.com/2011/03/forbes-400-best-way-to-build-wealth.html March 16 2011

2. UBS Investor Watch "Analyzing investor sentiment and behavior", p2 https://www.ubs.com/content/dam/WealthManagementAmericas/documents/investor-watch-3Q2013-report.pdf 2013

3. UBS Investor Watch "Analyzing investor sentiment and behavior", p2 https://www.ubs.com/content/dam/WealthManagementAmericas/documents/investor-watch-3Q2013-report.pdf 2013

4. UBS Investor Watch "Analyzing investor sentiment and behavior", p2 https://www.ubs.com/content/dam/WealthManagementAmericas/documents/investor-watch-3Q2013-report.pdf 2013

5. Marketing Mastery "Forbes 400 Best Way to Build Wealth" http://www.ourmarketingmastery.com/2011/03/forbes-400-best-way-to-build-wealth.html March 16 2011

6. Psalm 24:1 & Psalm 115:16

7. Luke 15:11-32

8. Proverbs 14:23

9. The Investor "Historical House Prices" http://monevator.com/historical-uk-house-prices/ January 5 2012

10. Romans 8.28

11. Habakkuk 2:2

12. Daniels, Peter J. How to be Motivated all the Time. Strathalbyn South Australia: World Centre for Entrepreneurial Studies, 1987. P45

www.ingramcontent.com/pod-product-compliance
Lightning Source LLC
Chambersburg PA
CBHW071410080526
44587CB00017B/3237